MOSCOW

PHILIP STEELE

WORLD ALMANAC® LIBRARY

Please visit our web site at: www.worldalmanaclibrary.com
For a free color catalog describing World Almanac® Library's list of high-quality books
and multimedia programs, call 1-800-848-2928 (USA) or 1-800-387-3178 (Canada).
World Almanac® Library's fax: (414) 332-3567.

Library of Congress Cataloging-in-Publication Data

Steele, Philip, 1948-
    Moscow / by Philip Steele.
        p. cm. — (Great cities of the world)
    Includes bibliographical references and index.
    ISBN 0-8368-5024-6 (lib. bdg.)
    ISBN 0-8368-5184-6 (softcover)
    1. Moscow (Russia)—Juvenile literature. [1. Moscow (Russia).] I. Title. II. Series.
DK601.2.S74   2003
947'.31—dc22   2003053474

First published in 2004 by
World Almanac® Library
330 West Olive Street, Suite 100
Milwaukee, WI 53212 USA

Copyright © 2004 by World Almanac® Library.

Produced by Discovery Books
Editor: Gianna Williams
Series designers: Laurie Shock, Keith Williams
Designer and page production: Keith Williams
Photo researcher: Rachel Tisdale
Maps and diagrams: Keith Williams
World Almanac® Library editorial direction: Jenette Donovan Guntly
World Almanac® Library art direction: Tammy Gruenewald
World Almanac® Library production: Beth Meinholz

Photo credits: AKG London: pp.7, 8, 10, 11, 27; AKG London/Keith Collie: p.33; Art Directors & Trip/Ask Images:
p.28; Art Directors & Trip/A. Semashko: p.36; Art Directors & Trip/A. Tjagny-Rjadno: pp.19, 29, 31, 34, 39, 43; Art
Directors & Trip/B. Turner: p.15; Art Directors & Trip/D. MacDonald: p.26; Art Directors & Trip/Eric Smith: p.4; Art
Directors & Trip/N & J. Wiseman: p.41; Corbis: pp.9, 24; Hutchison Library: pp.14, 42; Hutchison Library/Liba Taylor:
pp.18, 38, 40; Hutchison Library/Maurice Harvey: p.35; Hutchison Library/Robert Francis: cover, title page; Hutchison
Library/Vadim Krokhin: p.17; Novosti Photo Library (London): pp.22, 23; Panos Pictures: p.21; Panos Pictures/Caroline
Penn: p.25; Still Pictures: p.37; Still Pictures/Hjalte Tin: p.13; Still Pictures/Jecko Vassilev: p.20

Cover caption: Changing of the Guard at the Lenin Mausoleum in Moscow's Red Square.

Printed in the United States of America

1 2 3 4 5 6 7 8 9 07 06 05 04 03

Contents

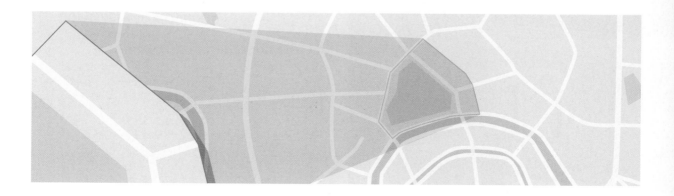

Introduction

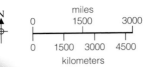

RUSSIAN FEDERATION

Moscow

KAZAKHSTAN   MONGOLIA

IRAQ IRAN   CHINA   JAPAN   PACIFIC OCEAN

INDIA

M oscow is the largest city in Europe. It is also the capital of the Russian Federation, the world's biggest nation. This single country takes in not only the plains and industrial cities of Eastern Europe, but also northern forests and Arctic lands. It includes the vast wilderness of Siberia, which extends right across northern Asia to the Pacific Ocean, and stretches south to Central Asia and China.

"Moscow seethes and bubbles and gasps for air. It's always thirsting for something new, the newest events, the latest sensation."

—Svetlana Alliluevya, writer, 1963.

◄ *Moscow's historic center is the Kremlin. Beyond its bell towers, churches, and former palaces, the modern city stretches to the horizon in a haze.*

Communism and Democracy

Between 1917 and 1991, Russia was part of the Communist Union of Soviet Socialist Republics (USSR), founded in 1922. Communism, a political ideology, asserts that all private property should be abolished and everything should be owned in common. In the Communist Soviet Union, health, housing, education, and jobs were provided for all citizens and run by the government.

Communism, however, also meant people could not own their own homes, and people had no choice but to use the products and services the government offered. The Russian people now elect a president and parliament. The parliament, called the Federal Assembly, consists of the Federation Council and the State Duma. Today, Russia is still struggling with the change from Communism to multiparty democracy.

CITY FACTS

Moscow
Capital of the Russian Federation

Founded: A.D. 1147

Area: 386 square miles
(1,000 square kilometers)

Population: 10,500,000
(2002 estimate)

Population Density:
27,202 people per sq mi
(11,945 per sq km)

When night is falling over Moscow, the sun is already rising over Russia's eastern islands. To best grasp the size of this country, go to Moscow's Yaroslavsky Station and board an express on the Trans-Siberian Railroad. It will be nearly a week—and seven of Russia's twelve time zones—before the train rolls into Vladivostok, on the Pacific coast.

Red Square

At the heart of old Moscow, Red Square borders the northwestern walls of the Kremlin, a 90-acre (36.4-hectare) area that contains the presidential palace and is the seat of Russia's government. The area now occupied by Red Square was cleared of housing over five hundred years ago by Czar Ivan III, called "Ivan the Great." It was used as a market square as well as a place of public executions and religious processions. It gained the name Red Square in the late 1600s and many famous events in Russian history took place there. In the Communist period, Red Square saw huge demonstrations and military parades. The body of the leader of the 1917 Communist revolution, Vladimir Lenin, is displayed in the Lenin Mausoleum there. Today, Red Square is thronged with tourists and is a venue for concerts and firework displays.

Principal Areas of Moscow (Inset of the Kremlin)

Beside the Moscow River

Moscow's Russian name is *Moskva*. A sprawling city, it is built around a river of the same name and linked by canal to the Volga River. The city's outer ring is a 67-mile (108-km) freeway.

In winter, Moscow has heavy snowfall and icicles hang from roofs. Cars speed through freezing slush. Muscovites wrap up in fur hats and big coats. The average January temperature is 14 °F (−10 °C). In summer, the weather becomes warmer and sunny, with temperatures often reaching 70 °F (21 °C) or more.

Moscow has many fine old buildings. At its center is the historic, red-walled citadel of the Kremlin. Inside the Kremlin is the bell tower of Ivan the Great, grand palaces, treasuries, cathedrals, and churches whose onion-shaped domes, in the Russian Orthodox style, gleam with gold. Across Red Square rise the multicolored domes of St. Basil's Cathedral.

Signs of Change

Over the ages, the city has grown outward from the Kremlin. The old city walls, then later boulevards and modern freeways, are all signs of the city's growth. They enclose green parks, as well as a wide range of building styles.

▼ *The Kremlin borders the Moskva (Moscow) River. The red walls of the old citadel enclose not only historic cathedrals, but the presidential offices of the Russian Federation.*

The Old Arbat region of the city features spacious houses of the 1800s, built when many artists lived in the district. However, there are also massive, often ugly, high-rise buildings dating from the 1930s and 1940s that housed government departments. Drab concrete apartments from the 1960s and factories with smoking chimneys stretch through the suburbs. Even there, however, ancient monasteries grace the streets.

CHAPTER 1

History of Moscow

Southwest Russia was the home of the Slavic people who make up most of the population of Moscow today. About 1,500 years ago, they spread northward and eastward and later conquered lands in Central Europe. Russia itself is named after the Rus, Swedish Vikings who founded communities in the region in the ninth century A.D. Small states developed from these settlements during the Middle Ages.

The first mention of Moscow in historic documentation is from 1147, when Yuri Dolgoruky, Prince of Suzdal—the capital of the region at the time and a major religious center—invited Prince Sviatoslav Olgovich of Novgorod, one of the oldest towns in Russia, to meet at a small, hillside settlement beside the Moscow River. This became Moscow, the capital of a state called Muscovy. It soon was topped by a wooden citadel, or "Kremlin," the timber replaced by stone in the 1300s. In 1325, Metropolitan Pyotr, head of the Russian Orthodox Church, transferred his seat to Moscow, making it the national religious capital.

Domination of the Mongols

At this time, the Russian states were repeatedly attacked by warriors from Central Asia known as Mongols. They forced the Russians to pay them money in tribute. In 1328, Ivan "Kalita," or

◀ *Czar Ivan IV ruled Russia for over thirty years. This painting can be seen in Moscow's Tretyakov Gallery.*

"Moneybags," was made grand prince by the Mongols. He collected tribute for them from other princes.

In 1380, the Muscovites revolted against the Mongols, who in retaliation burned Moscow to the ground. The Mongols' hold was finally broken by Ivan the Great (1462–1505), who made Muscovy the most powerful state in Russia. Moscow grew to become a city of 100,000 people, a place of towers, tolling bells, wooden houses, and muddy streets thronged with people.

Ivan the Terrible

Ivan IV, called "the Terrible," was the first to name himself czar, or "emperor," of all Russia. He conquered surrounding countries to increase his empire and built St. Basil's Cathedral, known also as the Cathedral of the Intercession.

The Czar Cannon

Visitors to the Kremlin today are amazed by the Czar Cannon, one of the biggest ever made. The 17-foot (5.3-meter) cannon weighs a remarkable 44 tons (40 tonnes) and features a 35-inch (890-millimeter) caliber bronze barrel. Created in the year 1586, the cannon features a picture of Fyodor, son of Ivan the Terrible.

"Now in these days [English merchants] have... made now and then promising voyages into... Muscovy... and the region whereabout, from which they bring home great commodities."

—William Harrison, author, 1577.

▼ St Basil's Cathedral, Moscow's best-known landmark, looks out over Red Square. Built for Czar Ivan the Terrible, it was completed in 1560.

Ivan the Terrible massacred thousands of people, including Russian nobles, and killed his own son in a rage. He died in 1584.

Romanov Moscow

In 1613, after a period of civil war and chaos, Mikhail Romanov came to the throne (his family would rule Russia until 1917). Peter I, "the Great," became czar in 1682, and decided to modernize his country. He built a new School of Navigation and Moscow's first theater on Red Square. He even made Muscovites shave off their long beards and told them how they should dress to make them look more European.

In 1712, Peter the Great moved the court from Moscow to St. Petersburg, the new capital he had built. Moscow, however, remained the commercial center of Russia and continued to thrive. Catherine "the Great" became empress in 1762. Under her rule, Moscow was transformed with new homes and bridges and paved streets. The population grew rapidly, despite a terrible plague in 1771.

War and Rebellion

In 1812, France invaded Russia and the French emperor, Napoleon, led his troops into Moscow. A great fire was started by

▼ *The fire that raged through Moscow in 1812 was followed by looting, a peasant uprising, and the retreat of Napoleon's troops.*

▲ *A giant Bolshevik towers over Moscow and the Lenin Library in this 1920 painting by Boris Kustodyev.*

Russian patriots, who burned the city down to prevent occupation. The French had no choice but to retreat through the freezing Russian winter. Although the retreat was a major factor in Napoleon's fall from power, Moscow had to be almost entirely rebuilt.

During the 1800s, the Romanov czars blocked political reforms. Ordinary Russians had few freedoms, and many lived like slaves. A suppressive and often cruel secret police was established, and rebels were exiled to distant Siberia. Alexander II, the only czar who tried to bring about change, was assassinated in 1881. By this time, Moscow was ringed with factories, while its tenements were filled with the poor and hungry.

In 1905, Russian protesters started an uprising and, to retain control, Czar Nicholas II was forced to create Russia's first parliament, but it had little power. The czar's rule was weakened further when, in 1914, a union of countries—the Central Powers (mainly Germany and Austria)—declared war (later named World War I) on the Allies, another alliance that included Russia. Multiple Russian military defeats and a great loss of life during the war caused a further lack of confidence in the czar and led to widespread domestic unrest.

Changing Names

Since the 1980s, many Moscow street names have been changed to reflect political changes. Old names honored Communist heroes such as Karl Marx. These have been replaced with the names of new heroes, such as the scientist and campaigner for reform Andrei Sakharov, or with old names from the time of the czars.

In March 1917, during a second uprising, the czar was overthrown. In yet another revolution (that November) the Bolsheviks, a Communist group, seized power after a week of intense fighting. Nicholas II and his family, held captive, were killed in 1918.

The USSR

The revolution of November 1917 was followed by a bitter civil war, won by the Communists. In 1918, Moscow was made the capital once more. Four years later, Russia became the dominant republic of the Union of Soviet Socialist Republics (USSR). Moscow became the capital of world Communism, an icon of either fear and mistrust or admiration for people around the world. In 1924, Soviet leader Vladimir Lenin died. He was replaced by Joseph Stalin, who ruled with the help of a brutal secret police. In 1928, Stalin drew up a plan to increase heavy industry, and Moscow became the center of a twentieth-century industrial revolution.

The Great Patriotic War

Despite a pact between Stalin and Nazi Germany, the Germans invaded the USSR in 1941 during World War II (known in Russia as the Great Patriotic War). Nazi troops advanced toward Moscow, where 450,000 Muscovites were digging trenches to defend the city. The Germans were beaten back and defeated by the Soviet Red Army, but 27 million Soviets died in the war, more than any other nation.

Postwar Reform and Turmoil

During the second half of the twentieth century, Muscovites longed for an improved standard of living, and for Western-style cars and consumer goods, but these were reserved for favored Communist officials. It was 1985 before the Soviet Union began to change, under the leadership of Mikhail Gorbachev, who brought in long-awaited political and economic reforms. Gorbachev began the Soviet Union's move toward democracy and a free-market economy.

The Communists made one last attempt to stay in power in 1991. Gorbachev was placed under house arrest, and tanks rolled through the streets of Moscow. Anti-Communist leader Boris Yeltsin rallied opposition near the Soviet White House (at that time the house of the parliament) and prevented the coup's leaders from gaining control. Climbing onto a tank, Yeltsin persuaded troops not to attack.

The Russian Federation

The 1990s saw democratic elections and rapid moves toward a capitalist economy. It also saw soaring prices, rising crime, and political chaos. People who seized opportunities created by the new free-market economy suddenly became extremely wealthy. With the onset of democratic reform, the Soviet Union fell apart. Many regions declared their independence. The largest of these was the new Russian Federation, with Boris Yeltsin

"This curious conglomeration of palaces, towers, churches, monasteries, chapels, barracks, arsenals, and bastions... are they not the whole history of Russia, the whole epic of the Russian nation?"

—Maurice Georges Paléologue, French ambassador to the Russian Court during World War I.

as president. In 1993, it was Yeltsin's turn to attack the White House. Rebels, including several government officials attempting to overthrow Yeltsin, were holding out there. Troops stormed the building, killing almost 150 people.

▼ Long lines for food and other basic supplies were a common feature of Communist Moscow. Shortages are still common today.

CHAPTER 2

People of Moscow

Only recently has there been any serious attempt to discover the true size of the population of Moscow. In 2002, the country held a census, the first since 1989, and the first in the Russian Federation's history. The actual population of Moscow is now estimated at 10.5 million people, much higher than previously thought.

Small Minorities

Most Muscovites are ethnic Russians, a Slavic people who make up 80 percent of the national population. The Russian language is spoken throughout the city, and all public signs are written in Russia's Cyrillic alphabet. "Moscow" itself is written "Москва."

Moscow's minorities include many of the 150 other ethnic groups to be found in the country. They include Tatars, Uzbeks, Armenians, Jews, Kurds, and Buryats. Other people belong to ethnic groups such as the Ukrainians, Belarussians, Georgians, or Azeris, whose homelands broke away from the old Soviet Union in 1990–91.

A small number of foreigners (less than 0.2 percent of the population) from Europe, North America, and Asia live in Moscow. They are mostly diplomats, businesspeople, those in the tourism industry, and students.

Life in Moscow has become even more of a challenge than ever since the fall

◄ *Muscovites love ice cream* (morozhenoe) *even when the weather is freezing.*

Marriage in Moscow

Various rituals are popular among newlyweds in Moscow. Couples may go to the Sparrow Hills to have their photograph taken against the backdrop of the city. Many visit the Tomb of the Unknown Soldier in the Alexander Gardens, below the Kremlin walls, and leave a bouquet of carnations by the eternal flame (above). The monument was unveiled in 1967 and commemorates the many Russians who died in World War II. At a time when many monuments of the Communist era have been removed or degraded, this memorial is still deeply respected. By visiting the tomb, newly married couples show their respect for the previous generations that made their happiness possible through sacrifice and suffering.

of Communism. Many social divides have opened up in recent years. The richest people in Russia live in Moscow, but there are also more desperately poor citizens than ever. Economic discontent has also led to a large rise in the number of people who hold extreme nationalist views. This in turn has lead to greater religious and ethnic intolerance. Occasionally, hatred has erupted into violence against minorities. Muslim Chechens face ill will in the capital as the republic of Chechnya, in the

Caucasus region, has been fighting a ten-year war of independence against the Russian government. Chechen rebels also have been responsible for numerous acts of terrorism in Moscow, heightening tension.

Religion in Moscow

Moscow has been the headquarters of the Orthodox Church in Russia, part of the Eastern Orthodox tradition, for nearly seven hundred years. Inside its historic cathedrals, churches, and monasteries are bearded priests, the smell of incense, flickering candles, and holy images called icons. Russian religious music is made up of chanting and a deep, swelling chorus.

Politics and the Church

For seventy years, the Christian religion was actively suppressed by the Communist authorities. The Orthodox Church had always been closely linked with the czars and had opposed political reform, placing it at odds with the new Soviet ideology. Under Stalin, many of Moscow's churches were closed or demolished. Many Muscovites continued to shun the church even after the fall of Communism in 1989–91. However, during the following four years, there was a rapid revival of Christian worship, with over 250 churches reopening. Now, 66 percent of Muscovites describe themselves as Orthodox, higher than the national average. About 20 percent attend church at least once a month.

Protestant, Catholic, and Uniate Christian groups are also present in the city.

There are many Orthodox churches in Moscow, including the Cathedral of the Assumption and the Cathedral of Saint Michael the Archangel, each with five gilded domes. The Cathedral of the Annunciation, built between the fifteenth and sixteenth centuries, boasts nine gilded domes, while St. Basil's Cathedral, with eight multicolored domes and a majestic central spire, graces one end of Red Square.

Orthodox Festivals

The most important Christian festival of the year is the Orthodox Easter, or Paskha. Moscow's churches are filled with the sound of chanting and worshipers exchange age-old greetings: "Christ is risen," ("Khristos voskres" in Russian) and "He is risen indeed,"

The Old Calendar

Russia's Christmas holiday takes place in January. Students of Russian history may be puzzled that the revolution of November 1917 is called the October Revolution. The reason for these differences is that the Russian Church did not accept changes made to the calendar by Roman Catholic Pope Gregory XIII in the 1580s, and so the dates vary. Today, only religious festivals and historic events are scheduled by the old calendar. In everyday life, people use the common Western calendar.

(*Voistinu voskres*). In the summer, Trinity Sunday (*Troitsa*) combines several holidays. The graves of family members are tidied, and houses and churches are decorated with birch branches to celebrate the growing season. Russia's Christmas celebration (*Rozhdestvo*) begins at midnight on Christmas Eve, January 6 on the Orthodox calendar. Each congregation joins a candlelit procession around its church.

Other Religions

Ten percent of the Russian Jewish population lives in Moscow, and the city has twelve synagogues. The capital's main synagogue, the Moscow Choral Synagogue, was built in 1891. In May 2001, Moscow Jews celebrated the restoration of its dome and gilded Star of David, more than a century after a czar ordered them removed.

Although one million Muslims live in Moscow, there are only six mosques. Founded in 1904, the Cathedral Mosque of Moscow is the headquarters of the Religious Board for Muslims of European Russia.

In recent years, many "cults," or new religious movements, have attracted small numbers of followers. Their popularity has been fueled by discontent with the country's economic state.

◄ *A priest leads Easter services at the Danilovsky Monastery, founded by Prince Daniil over seven hundred years ago. It has been the headquarters of the Russian Orthodox Church since 1988.*

▲ Char-grilled kebabs (shashlyk) *are served up in Moscow's biggest park, Izmaylovo. The dish came to the city from the Caucasus region and Central Asia.*

Food in Moscow

Moscow is probably more internationally famous for its alcoholic beverages, like vodka, than for its food. Nevertheless, Russia has a very distinctive style of cuisine.

A Moscow breakfast (*zavtrak*) might be a hurried cup of black tea and a crust of rye bread before work. However, breakfast might also include porridge (*kasha*) or pancakes (*bliny*), both made from buckwheat; soft-boiled eggs; or curd cheese (*tvorog*). Lunch (*obed*) is the main meal of the day in the home. Cabbage soup (*shchi*) is

often served, accompanied by sour cream. Beet soup (*borscht*), meat, and fish are other common lunchtime dishes. Gherkins, cold meats, or saltfish (salted cod) are popular choices for supper, which is generally a lighter meal.

Dining Out

Since the 1990s, foreign foods and quick takeout items such as hamburgers and pizzas have become popular in Moscow, alongside more traditional snacks, such as pancakes, sold by street vendors. Expensive restaurants and hotels serve lavish banquets in the evening to large parties of family or friends. The Hotel Metropol, a stone's throw from Red Square and just across the road from the Bolshoi Theater, houses a spectacular and extremely expensive restaurant.

There are all kinds of other eating places, down to the very cheap cafeterias, or *stolovaya*, which serve plain, filling food. For the poor, who are hungry on freezing winter nights, volunteers ladle out hot soup.

A Stiff Drink

Russia's most popular alcoholic beverage is vodka, a fiery spirit made from wheat and rye. It may be plain or flavored with herbs and spices. The finest vodkas are made in Moscow. Russian-produced beers, wines,

"Most Russians don't care whether they are ruled by fascists or Communists or even Martians as long as they can buy six kinds of sausage in the store and lots of cheap vodka."

—Alexander Lebed, Russian general and presidential candidate, 1994.

champagnes, and cognacs are also plentiful. Popular nonalcoholic beverages include coffee and black tea. Traditionally, the water for the tea is boiled in a tall, often elaborate, brass urn called a *samovar*.

▼ *The elegant, one-hundred-year-old Hotel Metropol serves as a luxurious backdrop for the excellent meals available in the hotel's restaurant.*

CHAPTER 3

Living in Moscow

Under Soviet rule, housing was provided by the government, rather than being owned by individuals or private property companies. Apartments in large concrete buildings were small and crowded, with cheap fixtures and few luxuries.

After 1992, Russians were allowed to buy and sell their apartments. Property companies bought up housing stock and forced prices to rise. At the same time, charges for electricity and other utilities soared. This left many elderly people, who only had small pensions from the government, struggling to survive. Though still a problem in much of Russia today, the effect of rising costs has not been felt so severely in Moscow, where prices and housing have been kept under some control.

Rich and Poor

Wealthy businesspeople, politicians, and bosses of criminal gangs built luxurious mansions around Moscow in the 1990s. These are surrounded by large grounds, enclosed by high fencing, and patrolled by security guards. By way of contrast, many poor people come to the capital in a vain search for work. Homeless, they have to sleep on the streets of Moscow if they cannot find shelter. The cold winter can mean death for the most vulnerable of the close to 100,000 homeless Muscovites.

◄ *Homeless people of all ages survive on the streets of Moscow, including many children.*

The Dacha

On summer weekends and during much of August, many Muscovites leave for the countryside and forests outside the city. There they own a *dacha*, or summer house. This may be a comfortable house or cabin, or little more than a shed with a small garden plot. Homegrown food and forest mushrooms are a lifeline for many families.

Staying Healthy

Political shifts have meant change in many aspects of daily life for Muscovites,

▲ Block after block of tall apartment buildings stretch to the horizon in this view of Moscow.

The Age of Elegance

Many of Moscow's houses were burnt down in the great fire of 1812, when Napoleon attacked the city, but a few streets of fine mansions survived the destruction. Along Volkhonka Ulitsa, for example, stand the elegant former homes of the noble families of the eighteenth and nineteenth centuries.

including health care. There are now private health-care services in Moscow as well as a government-run medical service. The average pharmacy, or *apteka*, will also offer advice on a wide range of health issues. Although there are many good nurses and doctors, many hospitals face shortages of both medicines and medical staff and much of their equipment is old-fashioned.

Since 1990, the average life expectancy for adults has become shorter. Indeed, Russian males now have the lowest life

Bathing in Style

Because bathing is believed to cure or relieve a host of medical conditions, many Muscovites visit a Russian banya, *or public bath house, quite regularly. A banya is somewhat like a sauna, with cold plunges, warm baths, and clouds of steam. Traditionally, bathers beat their skin with birch twigs to increase circulation. Many establishments also offer body massages, tea, herbal infusions, or alcohol. The baths offer a chance to socialize, as about fifty people may gather at one time. Men and women bathe separately.*

Some old bath houses are lavishly decorated. The Sandunovsky Baths (above right) on Neglinnaya Street are palatial. Built in 1806 and rebuilt in 1896, many famous people have passed through its doors, including writers Leo Tolstoy and Anton Chekhov. Two-hour sessions cost between $10 and $20.

expectancy in Europe at just fifty-nine years of age. Women can expect to live longer, but only to seventy-two. The annual death rate—of sixteen per one thousand citizens—is the highest in Europe.

The reasons for health problems are many and varied and are often related to the widening gap between rich and poor. Russia's population growth is in sharp

▲ *Although city hospitals may have shortages of drugs, most pharmacies now stock a fair range of imported medicines for day-to-day needs.*

decline, although the number of citizens in Moscow is rising as people move to the capital for its higher standard of living and potential for work.

Alcoholism is a long-standing problem in Moscow; many risk poisoning by making their own vodka, which can be lethal. More recently, drugs have ruined many lives and sharing needles has spread HIV/AIDS. Health officials recently announced that Russia may soon equal or surpass the United States in HIV-positive citizens. Muscovites comprise the largest portion of the more than 200,000 HIV-positive Russians.

Many Muscovites suffer, too, from breathing problems brought about either by heavy smoking or by air pollution. In the fall of 2002, Moscow was shrouded in dense smog. The authorities blamed forest fires around the city, but the recent increase in traffic also may have played its part.

Despite all these problems, many Muscovites like to keep fit. There are many gyms and jogging is popular in the city's parks.

Going Shopping

In their day, the aim of Moscow's Communists was to provide cheap food and other basic needs. Electrical appliances or cars were seen as luxury items and were very expensive. Clothes were cheap, but were

ПЛАТКИ · ШАРФЫ

КОЖГАЛАНТЕРЕЯ

GUM

GUM (*above*) is the most famous place to shop in Moscow. Its arcades date back to the 1890s. In 1917, it was taken over by the government and received its name (the initials stand for State Department Store). It was put to other uses under Stalin, but reopened as a store in 1952. Famous for its empty shelves, lack of choice, and long lines, it was returned to private ownership in 1993. Today, it is a mall of fashionable boutiques.

also dull and unfashionable. Shopping, even for basic groceries, could involve hours of standing in line. Shortages were common.

Today, all kinds of goods, many of them imported, are available around Red Square and within the Garden Ring, the wide, circular freeway in Moscow that carries heavy traffic. There are department stores, small stores, and supermarkets. Fashion outlets and perfumeries do a thriving trade. The freezing winter climate makes warm clothing essential. Furs and heavy outer clothing always have been worn by Muscovites, but today more and more people follow Western fashions. Those who cannot afford expensive items enjoy window shopping and buy their clothes secondhand.

Street Markets

Many Muscovites do their shopping for electrical and household goods, watches, perfumes with fake brand names, and

▼ Traders sell motor oil on a road outside the city. Muscovites do much of their shopping at markets and bargain sales rather than in the city's stores.

other goods at open-air markets. There are large street markets, too, for fresh produce, as on Danilovsky Street or Basmannyy Street. The biggest "flea market" is held in Izmaylovo Park on weekends. Here, there are all kinds of secondhand goods, even parts for cars. Also on sale in the park are arts, crafts, handmade clothes, and antiques.

Education

The first of September marks the start of a new school year in Moscow. Children traditionally bring bunches of flowers for their new teacher. During the Soviet period,

all school children wore the same uniform. Today, some Moscow schools have abolished uniforms, while others have brought in uniforms designed specifically for their own school. Typical school hours last from 8.30 A.M. until 3:00 P.M. The school year lasts through May, though several weeks in June are spent in exams.

Russian children must attend elementary and high school for at least nine years. There are plans to extend this period in future. High school classes include Russian

history, literature, and language, as well as foreign languages, math, and science. There is less central control of the curriculum than in the old days, with many schools specializing in certain areas.

The old Soviet education system was strict, but it produced well-qualified students. Economic problems in the 1990s led to drastic cuts in money spent by the government on schools, buildings, and equipment. Some wealthy parents now send their children to expensive kindergartens and private schools. The richest may even send their children to elite schools overseas.

▼ *It is the first day of a new term and the children have brought in bunches of flowers for their teacher.*

Moscow Conservatory

One of the most important music schools in the world, the Moscow Conservatory was founded in 1866. Over the ages, its teachers included such famous names as Pyotr Ilyich Tchaikovsky and Dmitry Shostakovich. Notes from Tchaikovsky's music decorate the railings in front of the building. The Conservatory's most famous pupil was Sergei Rachmaninov, the great composer of piano music who later made his home in the United States.

After School

Moscow can be a great city for children, with an abundance of theme parks, fairgrounds, a children's theater, and a long tradition of puppetry and circuses.

▼ *Moscow State University was constructed between 1949 and 1953 in the grandiose style admired by Stalin. Teaching takes place in the massive main building, while student halls occupy the wings.*

In the Alexander Gardens, below the Kremlin walls, children go sledding or throw snowballs in winter. In the parks in summer, in-line skaters and skateboarders roll through the grounds.

Higher Education

Moscow has more than seventy-five colleges and universities, and over seven hundred scientific institutions, including the Russian Academy of Sciences. Moscow's first university, Moscow State University (MGU), dates back to 1755. Its campus surrounds a tall skyscraper on the Sparrow Hills, overlooking the city. Though it is growing, with over 30,000 students, the university has had many problems with funding since the 1990s and some research programs have been canceled.

CHAPTER 4

Moscow at Work

During the Soviet period, Moscow was the center of government control over the country's economy. When government control was replaced by free-market capitalism during the 1990s, the changes were faster and more drastic in Moscow than elsewhere in Russia. The results were often chaotic and caused great hardship to Muscovites. Prices soared and then, in 1998, came an economic crash. International bankers had to come to the rescue.

However, the Russian Federation remains hugely rich in natural resources and, as the biggest country in the world, it will always be a central player on the world stage. During the Communist era, factories became outmoded and inefficient, because there was no competition from private firms to force improvements. Today, Russian industries must compete with firms from around the globe and have to improve the methods they use to produce goods.

Over half of all foreign investment in the Russian Federation comes to Moscow, making the capital the powerhouse of the Russian Federation. Today, 25 percent of all income in Russia is concentrated in Moscow, compared to only 10 percent in 1990. Outside of Moscow, only one-fifth of all Russians earn more than $70 a month. In contrast, more than half of all Muscovites earn more than $70 a month. This means

◀ *Builders at work in front of the Cathedral of Christ the Savior, rebuilt between 1995 and 1997.*

that the economic gap between Moscow and other regions of Russia has increased.

Industries

Moscow's industries include chemical, iron and steel production; oil refining; engineering; aerospace design; food processing; and vehicle manufacturing. Textiles, garments, and footwear also are produced in Moscow. Raw materials used in manufacturing, such as timber, minerals, or cotton, often must be transported to Moscow by rail over very long distances from Siberia or Central Asia.

Some three thousand factories or other industrial plants, such as oil refineries, are located in the city and its suburbs. There are also twelve power stations. These, along with traffic fumes, create severe air

▲ *A worker at the Chelnok factory makes fabric for footwear used by the army.*

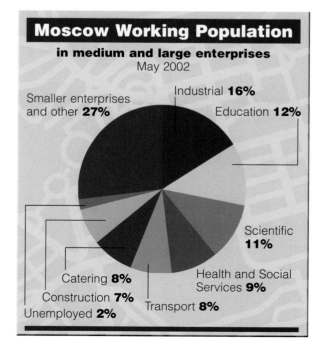

Moscow Working Population
in medium and large enterprises
May 2002

Smaller enterprises and other **27%**

Industrial **16%**

Education **12%**

Scientific **11%**

Health and Social Services **9%**

Transport **8%**

Catering **8%**

Construction **7%**

Unemployed **2%**

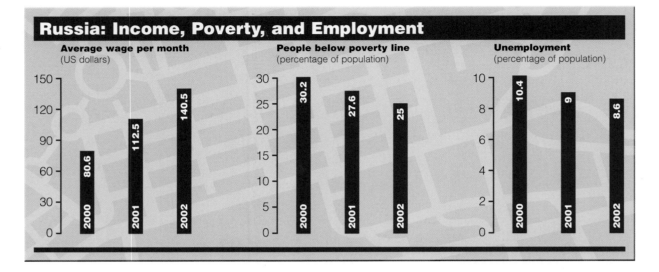

Russia: Income, Poverty, and Employment

Average wage per month (US dollars)
- 2000: 80.6
- 2001: 112.5
- 2002: 140.5

People below poverty line (percentage of population)
- 2000: 30.2
- 2001: 27.6
- 2002: 25

Unemployment (percentage of population)
- 2000: 10.4
- 2001: 9
- 2002: 8.6

▲ *Wages are going up and Russia is seeing a constant reduction in unemployment and poverty.*

pollution from sulfur dioxide, carbon monoxide, and other chemicals. The problem is worsening. Since the 1990s, however, air, rain, and snow quality have been carefully monitored. The official aim is to achieve clean air in Moscow by 2010.

A Worker's Life

Working conditions, safety standards, and industrial pollution are all serious problems. Wages are low, forcing many people to take on second or even third jobs. The highest paid employees work in private companies,

▼ *Although wages are low compared with other Western countries, they are increasing rapidly.*

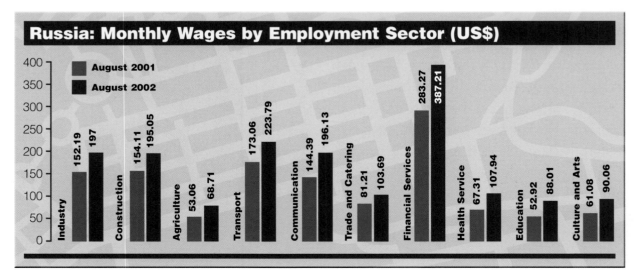

Russia: Monthly Wages by Employment Sector (US$)

■ August 2001
■ August 2002

Sector	August 2001	August 2002
Industry	152.19	197
Construction	154.11	195.05
Agriculture	53.06	68.71
Transport	173.06	223.79
Communication	144.39	196.13
Trade and Catering	81.21	103.69
Financial Services	283.27	387.21
Health Service	67.31	107.94
Education	52.92	88.01
Culture and Arts	61.08	90.06

particularly modern service industries like marketing firms. Among the worst paid workers in Moscow are teachers, who only earn $117 a month.

Moscow Media
Communication media has been at the center of change in Moscow since the 1990s. Although the presses are no longer run by the government in Moscow, the capital is still the chief center of publishing and broadcasting for the Russian Federation. The old Communist newspapers have been taken over by private companies or outstripped by tabloids and magazines.

Newspapers
Moscow-based daily newspapers include the *Kommersant* (the leading business-oriented newspaper), *Nezavisimaya Gazeta*, *Segodnya*, and *Komsomolskaya Pravda*. Moscow's own city newspapers include the *Moskovsky Komsomolets* and the *Kapital*, a weekly newspaper. English-language papers are published in Moscow, as well, such as the *Moscow Times*, the *Moscow Tribune*, and the *Moscow News*, which has a Russian-language edition called the *Moskovskie Novosti*.

Broadcast Media
Moscow is also the center of government-owned and commercial radio and television

◄ *Muscovites stop to buy newspapers and magazines. Today, they have a wide range to choose from.*

Free Speech?

There is no long-standing tradition of free speech in Russia. Today's reporters covering politics and crime find themselves under heavy pressure from government, business, or criminal interests not to publish or broadcast certain items of news. In 2001, an independent Moscow television station called NTV, which had criticized the government, was taken over by a government-run monopoly called Gazprom and many NTV journalists were fired. Some of these journalists went to work for another independent channel called TV-6. In 2002, this channel, too, came under legal and financial threats from a company closely linked to the government. The station was eventually forced to close.

stations, and a base for satellite TV companies. About 80 percent of Russian households own a color television set and this is the country's chief source of news. Popular viewing includes game shows and sports. There is concern that different sections of the media might fall under the ownership of the same small number of companies, which could potentially threaten the development of free speech.

New Media

The ownership of personal computers and mobile phones in Moscow is low by international standards, but in 2002, a report forecast that Internet use was set to grow by 40 percent in the near future. The Internet has made it much easier for people to access information directly.

Getting Around

Traveling around Moscow is becoming more of a problem with every year that passes. Car ownership has tripled since 1990, and now one in every five families has a car. Experts put the number of cars in Moscow at two million.

A ride to the city center can be expensive. The streets are busy, and there are taxis, minibuses, full-sized buses, streetcars, trolleybuses, and crowds of pedestrians. Winter driving conditions are icy and drivers use studded tires on their vehicles for safety.

The Metro

The best way to travel around the city is on the Metro, Moscow's subway system. Between 8 and 9 million people travel on the Metro's eleven lines, 160 stations, and 7,800 trains every day. Construction on the Metro began in 1931 and its first line opened in 1935. Currently, there are eleven lines, with more to come. Stations are marked above ground by a big red "M."

The Metro is cheap, clean, and runs trains very promptly. What is more, its stations' architecture is fascinating. Many have ornate designs and fittings dating back to the 1930s and 1940s. Some have tiled floors, marble pillars, pictures of heroic revolutionaries, and even statues.

By Air and Rail

Moscow has five airports. Its chief international airport, Sheremetyevo 2, was completed in 1980 and is about 17 miles (28 km) to the northwest of the city's center. Moscow's nine large railroad stations ring central Moscow, with trains from Europe pulling in at Belorussky, Leningradsky, or Kievsky stations. There is also a large suburban rail network.

National Government in Moscow

Russia is called the Russian Federation because it has a federal structure. This means that each of its regions or republics

▲ *This is not a palace or a luxury hotel, but a Metro station, complete with a vaulted ceiling, chandeliers, and ornamental arches.*

has its own elected local government, in addition to the national government, just as states do within the federal structure of the United States. Within the government, the city of Moscow has equal status with the republics of the Federation.

Moscow is the seat of government for the whole Russian Federation. The national parliament, or Federal Assembly, currently meets in a large 1930s building on Manezh Square, near the Kremlin.

Traffic Cops

A special branch of the police deals with road traffic. Its officers are officially known as the GIBDD or, more commonly, the GAI (State Inspectors of Traffic Safety). They pull over vehicles for all sorts of checks and can impose on-the-spot fines for minor offenses. However, this is sometimes seen as a useful source of private income by poorly paid police officers. It is against the law to drink any alcohol whatsoever before driving, but it is not unknown for drivers to pay a bribe to the police before they go out for the evening to keep from being stopped on the way home.

▲ *Passengers travel by trolleybus on a cold Moscow morning. Trolleybuses, streetcars, and buses run from 5 A.M. to 1 A.M. along routes not covered by the Metro.*

City Government

City Hall, a high-rise tower in the New Arbat district, is the city's second political power base. Moscow's own elected assembly, the City Duma (city parliament), is based there. The City Duma is presided over by a mayor, elected every four years, who has sweeping powers over the city's government. Eager to control its own affairs, the city government sometimes clashes with the national government and the Russian Federation's president.

▲ *The lobby of the State Duma, the Russian Federation's parliament, based in Moscow.*

The Mayor

Since 1992, the office of mayor has been held by Yuri Luzhkov. Luzhkov, nicknamed the "Czar of Moscow," is no lover of the ethnic minorities living in the capital and has whipped up public feelings against the Chechens. He has close links with business, and has set up grand—and expensive—building projects. However, Luzhkov has also ensured that the city functions and that the roads are repaired. He has been hugely popular with Muscovites, because they see him as someone who gets things done.

Successes and Failures

Moscow has always fascinated visitors. In the early 1920s, people saw a city in turmoil that was trying to shift from the Middle Ages to the Industrial Age in just a few years. In the 1990s, Moscow drastically changed its economy and tried to become a capitalist country almost overnight.

In reality, it takes many years to bring about major economic changes. The creation of a free economy without government controls opened the door to crime and corruption, which became widespread in business and government and affected everything from exports to political favors. Foreign businesses setting up in

Rebuilding the Cathedral

One of Moscow Mayor Luzhkov's pet projects has been the rebuilding of the Cathedral of Christ the Savior (below) in Moscow. The original, which was built between 1839 and 1883, was destroyed by Stalin in 1931.

The cost of the restoration was about $360 million. Architects doubted whether the rebuilding was worthwhile and many others felt the money should have been spent on more pressing problems.

Moscow bribed officials in order to gain contracts. Companies still get away with trading unfairly. Even street market traders must pay "protection" money to gangsters or be beaten up.

Regulations were instituted, but they failed to resolve the problem. Some Muscovites complain that stories of corruption are exaggerated by anti-Russian news reporters in the West, or that it is no longer common. However, in 2002, the president of the Russian Federation, Vladimir Putin, admitted that corruption at all levels was still seriously damaging the economy.

Crime and Deprivation

Both federal and city governments have so far failed to deal with Moscow's big problems, such as poverty and homelessness. Since Communist times, incidents of racially motivated crime have soared. Domestic violence is common. Gangs ruin countless lives by dealing drugs. About 6 percent of fifteen- to sixteen-year-olds in Moscow admit to having used heroin. President Putin has called the battle against drug addiction "a fight for the survival of the nation." In this war, Moscow is the key battleground.

Good News

There is some evidence, however, that progress is being made in Moscow's fight against crime. The city is better policed than other large Russian cities. Despite all the serious problems, the changes of the last ten years have transformed Moscow. The lights are on in the shops and the cafés. People can and do speak their minds. The people of Moscow are enjoying their new freedoms.

The change in the cultural climate has also been noticeable in the number of

"To visit Moscow in the five years since the collapse of Communism and the Soviet state is to be thunderstruck on a daily basis."

—David Remnick, American writer, 1997.

tourists that visit the capital. In 1999, 2.5 million people visited Moscow, one million of them from outside the Russian Federation. The World Tourism Association has predicted that by 2020, Moscow will be the fifth most popular city destination for tourists in all of Europe.

▼ *American businesses started appearing in Moscow as soon as the Cold War ended. McDonald's restaurant opened in the city in 1990 and there are now a dozen branches.*

CHAPTER 5

Moscow at Play

M oscow has long been a cultural capital of the world. This is a reputation the city is clinging to in spite of political and economic turmoil. The Russian State Library probably ranks second in the world both in size and facilities behind the Library of Congress (in Washington, D.C.). The Central Exhibition Complex comprises seventy-two pavilions showcasing industry, agriculture, science, and culture. Adjoining its landscaped grounds are the Russian Academy of Sciences Botanical Gardens.

Performing Arts

Moscow is a city of concert halls and music schools. The Bolshoi Theater, built in the 1800s, is Moscow's oldest theater. It serves as home for the Bolshoi Ballet Company, the world's greatest ballet company from the 1950s to the 1970s, though it has been hit by financial problems since the 1990s.

Muscovites are great lovers of drama and the capital has over 125 theaters. Many of them were built around Teatralny Proezd— or "Theater Square"—in the Tverskaya district. The Moscow Arts Theater had close links with Anton Chekhov, one of the world's greatest dramatists. Moscow is also the center of the Russian film industry and hosts an international film festival every other summer.

◄ *Enormous chandeliers hang from the opulent Hall of Orders in the Great Kremlin Palace.*

▲ *Plays by Anton Chekhov are always popular at the Moscow Arts Theater. Chekhov wrote especially for this company and married one of its actresses.*

Art Museums and Palaces

Moscow is rich in distinguished art. Museums, such as the old Tretyakov Art Gallery, the new Tretyakov Gallery in the Central House of Artists, and the Pushkin State Museum of Fine Arts, house both Russian and international masterpieces.

Both Tretyakov galleries concentrate on Russian art. In the old Tretyakov hang six-hundred-year-old religious icons painted by Andrei Rublev alongside realistic paintings, by Ilya Repin, chronicling Russian history.

The Pushkin Museum houses valuable international pieces by masters such as Renoir, Cézanne, and Matisse.

Moscow's palaces dazzle the eye with historic jewelry, fabrics, and furniture, including Granovitaya Palace, completed in 1491; Terem Palace, completed in 1636; and the Great Kremlin Palace, completed in 1849, all part of the Kremlin complex. The sixteenth-century palace of the Romanov Boyars (Russian nobles) is also impressive.

Rite of Spring Festival

Moscow today is becoming a lively center of modern performance and visual arts, with open-air concerts of jazz and pop music. The Vesenniy Obryad, or Rite of Spring Festival, held in March celebrates experimental arts.

Moscow's Parks

Summer in Moscow is the time for sunbathing in open spaces or swimming in the Moscow River. Every city needs its green spaces, and parks play an important part in Moscow life and leisure.

The Alexander Gardens, in the shadow of the Kremlin, feature statues of well-known characters from Russian fairy tales. Gorky Park, near the Moscow River, is probably the city's most famous park. It features amusement parks and popular walking paths.

East of the city, along a street called Shosse Entuziastov, lies Izmaylovo Park. The 740-acre (300-hectare) park surrounds the seventeenth-century Church of the Intercession in Izmaylovo.

In the western part of the city, Park Pobedy (Victory) commemorates the Great Patriotic War (World War II). A famous triumphal arch remembering the events of 1812 also has been moved to this site.

Outdoor Activities

The Russians have a passion for chess and it is often played in the open air in Moscow's parks. In winter, the parks are also the place where amateur skaters take to the ice. A rink is even set up for a few days in Red Square. Many Muscovites like to go bowling, play tennis, or use gyms or swimming pools.

▶ *A woman braves the ice for a winter swim in the northern suburbs of Moscow.*

The city hosts two marathon races each year, while a sports complex occupies the site of the 1980 Olympic Games. Moscow also has several large sports stadiums and offers horse racing at the Hippodrome.

Popular Teams

Though not often associated with Russia, baseball is actually a very popular game in Moscow. In fact, Russians claim that

▲ *Gorky Park, also known as Park Kultury, includes three amusement parks and many popular trails.*

baseball was invented there hundreds of years ago. The Moskvich, RusStar, and MGU Tornado teams are based in Moscow.

Soccer is one of the most popular spectator sports in Russia. The playing season lasts from March to November. Moscow's soccer clubs, which include Spartak, Lokomotiv, Dinamo, and CSKA, number among the leading teams in Europe.

Another Moscow passion is hockey. This sport peaks during the winter months, although its two top competitions, the Spartak Cup and the World Championships, take place in July and August.

City Festivals

In January, ice sculptures appear in Gorky Park for Moscow's Vjugovey Festival. Later in the season, Maslenitsa, or Pancake Week, celebrates the end of winter and the beginning of the Christian Lenten season. People cook pancakes (bliny), burn straw dolls, pick willow branches, and build snow forts. In September, people celebrate the founding of Moscow with fireworks, folk dancing, and parades.

CHAPTER 6

Looking Forward

All cities face an uncertain future, but in Moscow, this is especially true. The city has been on a roller-coaster ride of change in recent years. Many of the city's chief trading partners, such as Poland, are scheduled to join the European Union. The Russian Federation is becoming increasingly involved with western alliances such as the North Atlantic Treaty Organization (NATO), against the will of many of Moscow's nationalists.

In the past, too much centralization of power in Moscow proved disastrous. Today, profit from Russia's vast resources is still being spent mainly in Moscow. If wealth, political power, and justice are not spread more evenly throughout the Federation, Moscow will remain an island. Conflicts from other regions have already spilled over onto Moscow's streets.

The continuing war against the Chechens has already resulted in a severe terrorist backlash. In October 2002, a group of Chechen terrorists took an entire audience hostage in a Moscow theater. While trying to rescue the hostages, Russian troops killed 119 hostages and 50 terrorists.

Political Reform and Justice

Moscow's citizens are demanding that their politicians step up the fight against bureaucracy, corruption, crime, poverty,

◀ This young Muscovite, ready for the winter cold, has a bright future in the new Moscow.

poor housing, and poor health within the city itself. Instituting a system of social justice would likely ease other problems, such as racism and extreme nationalism, which sometimes lead to violence.

Building a New City

Bulldozers and cranes are creating a new city of Moscow. Plans are being made for the future, including a monorail line, a mini-metro line to serve the inner city, new shopping malls, offices, hotels, improved communication, and facilities to increase tourism. The city of heavy industry is becoming a city of services and international business.

In 2001, the Moscow City Government earmarked $11 million for renovating architectural complexes and historical places, improving transportation and medical services for tourists, building better

▲ *A new footbridge is constructed to cross the Moscow River. Better transportation and infrastructure are essential improvements to ensure future growth.*

tourist routes, and renovating hotels, as well as building new ones. There are currently 170 hotels in Moscow, the majority of which require serious repair work.

Over the ages, Moscow has survived attacks by the Mongols, the French, and the Germans. It has been burnt down more than once and rebuilt. A common thread runs through Moscow—a raw, vibrant energy and a toughness in the face of hard times. These impress the visitor to Moscow as much as the golden domes of its cathedrals or the walls of the Kremlin. These values, coupled with Moscow's unique culture, will see new generations of Muscovites reinventing their society and their city in the coming century and beyond.

Time Line

1147 Moscow is first mentioned. Yuri Dolgoruky of Suzdal confers with Sviatoslav Olgovich by the Moscow River.

1156 A wooden fortification is built on the present-day site of the Kremlin.

1238 Muscovy is conquered by the Mongols of Central Asia.

1328 Ivan I "Kalita" of Moscow is made grand prince by his Mongol overlords.

1380 Muscovy goes to war with the Mongols. Moscow is burnt to the ground.

1533 Ivan IV, "the Terrible," proclaimed czar (emperor).

1613 The start of the Romanov dynasty.

1682 Peter I, "the Great," becomes ruler and decides to modernize the country.

1712 St. Petersburg founded as the new Russian capital, but Moscow remains a center of power.

1812 French army takes Moscow. Russian patriots burn the city. The French retreat.

1905 Uprising in Moscow forces the creation of a parliament with little power.

1914 World War I breaks out. Russia is allied to France and Britain.

1917 Revolutions: Czar Nicholas II is overthrown in March; Communists seize power in November.

1918 Moscow becomes capital again; Nicholas II and his family are killed.

1922 The Union of Soviet Socialist Republics (USSR) is founded.

1924 Bolshevik leader Vladimir Lenin dies. Joseph Stalin comes to power.

1941 World War II begins for the Soviet Union as German army invades; Germans are eventually beaten back from Moscow.

1980 Moscow Olympics. Sheremetyevo 2 airport opens.

1985 New Communist leader Mikhail Gorbachev's reforms move Soviet Union toward a free-market economy.

1991 Anti-reformers seize power, lose it to Muscovites opposed to Communism. Collapse of Soviet Union; founding of Russian Federation. Boris Yeltsin is elected president.

1992 Yuri Luzhkov becomes Mayor of Moscow.

1993 Yeltsin attacks rebels in Russia's White House with tanks.

1997 Rebuilding of the Cathedral of Christ the Savior is completed.

2000 Vladimir Putin becomes Russian President.

2002 Chechen terrorists take theater audience hostage.

Glossary

arcades a group of shops that are connected by the arched ceiling of a covered walkway or avenue.

boulevards broad city streets, often with landscaped medians and surroundings.

bureaucracy a system of administration bogged down by an excess of paperwork, formalities, and regulations.

capitalism an economy based on private ownership and investment, and competitive free markets for goods and services.

census an official government report on a country's population.

centralization where power is concentrated into one place, rather than into smaller regions and groups.

Chechens people from the North Caucasus region of Russia. Chechnya declared its independence from Russia and the two sides are fighting a civil war.

citadel a city fortification or stronghold such as the Moscow Kremlin.

civil war fighting between two groups of citizens within the same country.

commodities raw materials, produced by agriculture or mining, that are transported from one part of the world to another and are bought and sold, such as oil and gas. The price of commodities affects the price of many other products in an economy.

Communist someone who believes that all property should be owned in common. A Communist government then controls the economy and all property.

curriculum a plan that sets out what students should learn each year.

Cyrillic alphabet the form of letters commonly used in Russia. The alphabet is named after St. Cyril, a ninth-century Greek monk who brought Christianity to the Slavs.

democracy government of officials who represent the will of the people and come to office in free elections held periodically.

Eastern Orthodox a form of Greek Christianity started in the Byzantine Empire of the fifth and sixth centuries. Still followed in Greece, Russia, and other countries, each branch is slightly different.

ethnic group a group of people sharing the same cultural background and language.

ethnic Russian a Slav of the Russian ethnic group. Citizens of the Russian Federation belong to many ethnic groups.

exiled someone forced to move to another region or to leave the country.

free-market economy when goods and services are bought and sold without controls or interference by the government, in hopes that competition will result in lower prices and higher quality.

HIV the virus that causes AIDS, a disease of the immune system.

ideology the ideas, beliefs, and aims that form a social and political system.

nationalist (1) someone who wants their country to govern itself or be independent; (2) someone who believes their own nation is superior to others.

occupation the seizure and settlement of a country by foreign military forces.

pollution the poisoning of the natural environment by industrial chemicals, exhaust fumes, or human waste.

tribute the forced payment of money or goods by a nation or its ruler to another nation or conqueror. The payment often signals submission or is paid in exchange for protection from other forces.

Further Information

Books

Hatt, Christina. Moscow (*World Cities*). *Thameside Press, October 1999.*

Kent, Deborah. *Moscow (Cities of the World).* Children's Press, March 2000.

Toht, Patricia. *Daily Life in Ancient and Modern Moscow (Cities Through Time).* Runestone Press, May 2003.

Vorhees, Mara. *Lonely Planet Moscow (Travel Guides).* Lonely Planet, March 2003.

Web Sites

www.interknowledge.com/russia/moscow01.htm
The Russian National Tourist Office site offers useful information about Moscow and its history.

www.museum.ru/gmii/maine.htm
Visit the Pushkin State Museum of Fine Arts site for museum information and pictures of its exhibits.

www.lonelyplanet.com/destinations/europe/moscow/index.htm
Lonely Planet offers Moscow travel and history information, and takes you "off the beaten track."

www.bolshoi.ru/eng/history.shtml
Explore the history of the famous theater and the ballet company it houses.

Index

Page numbers in **bold** indicate pictures.